The Tiger in the Vineyard

Michael Robinson

The Tiger in the Vineyard

Acknowledgements

Poems in this collection have appeared in the following journals:
Centoria, Five Bells, Hobo, Island, Poetry Matters, Studio;
and in *Prismatics: Poets Union Anthology 2008*, ed. John L. Sheppard
(Sydney: Poets Union, 2008).

'A Letter on Youth Homelessness' won
the 2009 Gwen Harwood Poetry Prize.

'On a Party in a Disused Prison' was runner-up
in the 2007 Tom Collins Poetry Prize.

The Tiger in the Vineyard
ISBN 978 1 76041 016 2
Copyright © text Michael Robinson 2015
Cover design: Jacqueline H. Telford

First published 2015 by
GINNINDERRA PRESS
PO Box 3461 Port Adelaide 5015 Australia
www.ginninderrapress.com.au

Contents

I	7
Angel in Chicago	9
On a Party in a Disused Prison	10
The Mystery of Good and Evil	12
Dolphins at Noon	14
A Letter on Youth Homelessness	16
The Order of Things	18
Streetwalker	20
The Double	21
The Theatre	23
The Chorus	24
Street Doctor	25
Wellington Square	27
The Conference	28
Letter to a Judge	30
II	31
Cemetery Beach	33
On an epitaph in the Nicholson Museum	34
After Horace, Ode 1.11	35
Mermaid	36
The Heron and the Moon	37
Performance Poem	38
Black Dog	39
The oldest woods	40
A Confession for Duns Scotus	41
The Fallen Tree	43
III	45
What is beyond the stars	47
Portrait of an Old Man	48

The Tiger in the Vineyard	50
Murderer and Child	51
Museum of Contemporary Art	53
The Painter	56
The Hanged Man	58
The Funeral Ship	61
The Sea Gods	65
Shopping for Clothes	66
The Stripper	68
Departure Lounge	69
A Fallen Soldier	71
An Emptiness of Rivers	73
The Silver Cylinder	74
The Northbridge Sculptures	75

I

Angel in Chicago

Winter mounts. But, magically, pears and strawberries,
Tender avocado, sweet red cherries,
Basil, coriander, rocket, lobster
Load down tables in the homeless shelter,
Until I brace my coat to meet the weather.
Towers turn above me. Bus and snowplough
Follow each other, groaning, through the ice.

What destiny has fallen on me now,
That I, who rub gloved palms and beg alone
And grant each passer-by who helps me grace,
Must stand amid the flames of Paradise,
The irrevocable judge, unseen, unknown,
Of all who worked and bled to build this place,
And pardon what I will, before God's face?

On a Party in a Disused Prison

Most of all for you, I can and should attend,
However cold the setting, no matter what books await
My contemplative moments – recognising the peace,
The world of bird and bottlebrush, rose, ibis, rain,
Conversation, company and light, the piercing joy

You give me. Together at a café table, talking; inching
Gradually south on a choked freeway, the railway's new growth
Frozen beside us; whether we watch dancers through clouds
Of noise on a club floor, users scoring heroin's
Deadly torpor, gulls caressing wind, wind and sand,

All around us is your caring, for daughters, colleagues, waifs
Wounded on sunlit roads, for friends your gentleness warms.
For friends – tonight for friendship's sake we mount wooden,
Freezing steps to the prison, enter the dreadful gate,
Cross the parade ground under limestone walls

Lined with ancient windows, barred, cold cages,
Pass down a narrow stair to the bowels of man-made hell,
To find the birthday party. These buildings where men existed
And fought, and men were hanged, speak decades of rape and death.
Stone crumbles to the touch, reveals rot in wood,

Old, wearied metal. Doors open on nowhere,
Balconies reach over emptiness. People stand smoking
And chattering, brittle generic blondes dance; the bar
Argues its vigorous trade. Tasteful electronic
Music mitigates the black void. We know people,

We talk, and sign the book. Some are in fancy dress,
Striped suits and arrows. Lines of long dead convicts
Walk unseen in drab prison green, follow departed
Nights' rituals of despair, wait for hoped visits
That may never have come. A security officer watches,

Peering over his belly, young women in brief,
Flared skirts, black stockings, deep-cut tops. There are speeches,
Creamy profiterole cake. We take our sociable leave,
Brush limestone dust from our coats, ascend the bitter stair,
Walk back past gate, iron, cell block, under sky

That has hidden the stars. Looking up at the dark,
The barred windows, I offer silent apologies
To what is here, will always be here, of all
Who suffered, justly or unjustly, with hope or without it,
Who died, in courage or despair, before the gate stood open.

The Mystery of Good and Evil

Plane trees elucidate the skyline with filigreed
Green starting from grey arms; grant
Boles, vulnerable havens, to magpie, lorikeet,
Nurturing their generations, nesting in secluded
Plain air. Though their pollen in spring
Chokes me, harvests my throat with hooks of fire,
If I sit outside at the tables where the drug dealers talk,
They humanise the street's dust, compound
Parking bays and the rehabilitation centre
With light's comfort. Old beyond their hours,
Combatants besiege the habit of dead years

Moment by moment through their cold trenches,
Throw idle balls in the shaded garden.
Thoughts are insubstantial and my mind recoils
From death-salinated pasts; word and grammar
Disintegrate into old etymologies; but we sit this morning
Over cappuccinos near the shattered glass door
While noon approaches the pavement. You give hope
To women who have none. Sisters are in prison
And you visit with empathy and new paths. Teachers
In training rooms are midwives at the birth
Of day from a womb of midnight. Old beyond her hours,

A customer chats with the dealers. One
Leans toward her; something changes hands. Pale and tall,
Grey like the dawn of a hanging, stiffly his partner
Checks whether I'm watching. Street-lined faces,
Old beyond their hours, follow her leaving. A once young man,
Unfolding his wallet, crosses the patient road
From the centre's youth reception. Posters
And paintings welcome the tables where your courses flow.
Cakes, pikelets and jams wait ready in the kitchen.
Odysseus warned Achilles never to send
His Myrmidons starving into battle.

Dolphins at Noon

1

In shadowy lunchtime light, at the corner table,
Four men in dark suits confer over pasta,
Steaks, salads, boutique beers, with a fifth,
Shaven-headed, in aged bikie leather.
Sun from the open door catches on half-full glasses.

2

Teenage drug users slump on the bright veranda
Of an iron-roofed house in a street of brothels,
Car yards, restaurants, adult cinemas. Down the corridor
Outreach workers gather. A nurse in a narrow room
Dispenses immunisations, fit-packs.

Posters bleed from the walls. Children's art-work
Cries out of poverty words about hepatitis,
Safe injecting, comforting each other
On the verge of death. Earth and a tree make
The garden. Music shrills. Young voices laugh.

3

We look over the boardwalk to the swelling water.
Coffee lingers. Gulls wait their chances
At abandoned meals. One darts in to scavenge.
Families fish from the long jetty. Masts and oars,
Gentle sea and sand, midday clarity.

Rippling waves move in from the naval island.
Minded, the waves might remember the first ships,
First stromatolites, coelacanths, driftwood ten million
Decades ago bleached white on sand already
Ancient, the first smugglers, first tears of loss.

But the sea has no mind. Above, behind, below,
Governing the sea, inscrutable decisions
Guide the weave of wave, plankton, shoal.
Children splash in clean shallows. Dolphin parent,
Dolphin child break the surface, gleam and play.

A Letter on Youth Homelessness

My friend, I write to wish you all that's true,
A prompt return to health and peaceful nights.
I trust your ex keeps faith, you keep your rights
To hearth and children. I shall think of you.
Myself, I read and sleep and try to work,
Endure bureaucracy and look for truth
To succour children in the growing murk
Of jail and homelessness – abandoned youth
Who grope for ways to live in swelling night,
Disintegrate in rage, or wake and fight.

At times it seems I'm in some clichéd game
Of post-apocalyptic dread and breakage.
A fallen civilisation's towers and wreckage
Cover a ruinous landscape, while in shame,
Bewilderment and violence, shattered bands
Move cursing through the pockmarked streets for scraps,
Dreaming of love and home in heartless lands
To justify their journey without maps.
And now and then we choose a child we find
In the rubble to feed, and leave thousands behind.

No, I exaggerate. The disinherited
Doubtless are always with us. But our age
Of cruelty and ignorance and the sage
Devourers of the light compels unmerited
Sufferings to the innocent in faster,
Harsher numbers. Lunar iron mines boom
And office towers rise from slabs, and master-
Planned communities burgeon, with no room
For Christ-child, homeless child, in the estate
Where bank and landlord gloat around the gate.

And still we work to help the folk we may
To see the almond blossom wake each spring,
And how the jasmine's petals gently sing
And rosemary evokes the ending day.
Young women come from prisons. Not all die.
Some learn to live again, and live to heal.
I watch them learn to walk with heads held high,
And now the lost and desperate reveal
Redemption. Now my library waits for me.
The jasmine, lavender. The opening tree.

The Order of Things

I walk alone and sleep on a filthy mattress
In a filthy squat. There are graffiti on the wall,
Images of loneliness, visions of distress
In the ruin of a civilisation. Infants call,
Alone and lost, through the rough shout of the stranger.
Choirs sing hosannas through the bottle's crash.
I bow my head among the fractured furniture,
Cracked chairs, a jarrah table scarred with ash.
Awake I dream, asleep I watch fresh day
Reach with its gold across fields far away.

I stroll around the art gallery because it's free,
Air-conditioned, sheltered when the hot winds blow.
Wandering from room to room, I see
Sadness, disintegration, frames that show
The twentieth century's madness, the twenty-first
Struggling in its wreckage. Then other displays,
Colour and harmony, symmetries of the sunburst,
And living gold of the Renaissance spreads its rays
Into shadows of empiricism, touches with faith
The newly glimpsed forest, the river's wraith.

Cubism deconstructs perspective, breaks
Passionate limbs and faces into planes,
Harsh lines, deep greens and browns. Futurism aches
To run the palpitating mind like trains
Gliding on gleaming rails into cold light.
Rusted, twisted metal and wire make sculptures,
Like the shattered factory I slept in, one grey night
Of rain and dreams. Realists read their lectures
Of politics, oppression and class war.
But now evening approaches. I make for the door,

Wondering where to go. I think of my friends
Waiting in graveyards or dispersed, dust, into air.
Saints robed in timeless music watch while time bends
Fragile lives into love, magic, despair
Or triviality. Time and space reveal
The roaring sea that sunders me from my fellows,
The streams I wade through, hoping for a meal
And a place to rest. The city's browns and yellows,
Its angry crimsons flash on banished souls,
Separate songs no counterpoint controls.

This is the order of things. Innumerable lives,
Each in the frame of others, all unique,
Burning and dying until the word arrives,
The word eternal joy and agony speak,
White flame of logic. Loneliness walks the streets,
Suffers where drivers crawl along darkening kerbs,
Hunting the ghosts of love. Heaven repeats
The quiet song that comforts and disturbs
My twilight wanderings, old trouble's shadows,
Empty roads, houses with boarded windows.

Streetwalker

As bereavement scores the tree's green gestures –

Her hands
Are the seams of mourning.

What glows in her look
Is a hidden road
To an orchard
Busy with apples.

Daughter of granite
And the green tides.

The Double

I saw my other self sitting alone,
A single cup of coffee growing cold.
He wore greasy jeans, a flannel shirt, old
Boots. His long hair straggled. The years had thrown
Him onto this time like beached wood, but aware.
  Beyond despair,
He waited for the next hit. Then eyelids drooped,
His head sank, and deadly reverie swooped.

Then I (my present self) looked at my twin,
Thinking how lives hold forks and falls of hail,
And how we grope through sun and night and trail
Calamity and loss. I can't begin
To judge you, unknown friend, although your breath
  Each day brings death
To those who trade with you and buy the shame
The years have made your world, in freedom's name.

What twists and turns, what troubles I have seen,
What failures. But my blessings grow like seasons
Restoring leafless boughs to blossom, reasons
Building from the ash of what has been
Old truths, new pathways founded on the light
  She gives. The sight
Of daily kindness. Thanks to her I rise
Each day accepted, welcome in her eyes.

When you're leaving hell, they say, don't look
Back, don't pause on the upward way. Keep
Your mind on the leaves and flowers, the steep
Shafts of sunlight, mossy steps, the brook
Running over stones. But I remember others,
 Sisters, brothers,
Dreaming at their tables, clutching crumbs
Of heroin, till the last withdrawal comes.

The Theatre

They built the sandstone theatre near the edge
Of the long desert, jagged with rocks and grey
Grasses, wine-red earth, an ancient day
Open to the towering heat. Earth's upper room.
Generations danced across the stage.
Light melodramas, comedies of gloom
Acted to entertain and feast our town.
Dancer, juggler, acrobat and clown
In jovial costumes, fresh applause and laughter,
Kindly humour, happiness ever after.

So we took our children. That was our first mistake.
They laughed and chattered, climbed up on their seats,
Squealed at trapeze artists, clapped to the beats,
Cheered the hero, booed the villain's pride.
Then the plots began to change. Dark heartache
Poured across the hall. The heroine died,
Groaning in pain. Ugly colours clashed,
Burning our eyes. Atonal music thrashed,
Rubbish fell from the wings and dealers prowled
The boards, and smoked while dying addicts howled.

Dismayed, we hurried outside and milled around
The cooling rocks. They towered red and high,
Streaked with iron. We heard a young boy's cry,
And knew our worst error was to leave them there,
Alone in the theatre of hate and brutal sound.
And now sweet children's echoes haunt the air.
We fan across the desert, tap the walls,
Search the aisles, the dressing rooms, the stalls,
And dream one day we'll find them. Lizards rush
Over the sand, and snakes rustle in the brush.

The Chorus

   Rain sounds on the soft street
   Outside the coroner's court.
We are the chorus, summoned and complete
With camera, notebook, microphone. We report
The morning's nightmares to the watching, reading
Millions hidden from us. Daily we hear
And never understand stories of bleeding,
Sighing souls and bodies. We draw near,
   Comment and move on.
   But death is long.

   Deaths are long, and lies.
   The cool marble wall,
The marble steps' pallor, emphasise
Time's impersonality. Past recall,
A woman's rage is silent, and her smile
Lost to the centuries. The grief she knew
Cremated with her flesh. The coroner's file
Records the proximate cause of death. A few,
   That know, won't tell,
   Keep secrets well.

   How shall our city live
   Now that such things pass?
Morning after morning we assemble, give
The truths we glean, like blades of bloodstained grass
From murderous fields, to soothe our audience.
The dead live, they are gathered to the sun.
All who dream past homelessness in silence
Died long ago. Their thoughts are lost, undone,
   Like wrinkled sheaves
   And crumpled leaves.

Street Doctor

Waiting for the doctors in Perth's evening light,
To talk, or tend their scars, or watch them fight,
Heal superficial ailments, mend hearts' grief,
Or sidling towards a drug dealer to buy
Dust under the plane trees and friendly chat,
To soothe old wounds with heroin's relief,
They show a courage stolid minds deny.
No parenting, no literate belief,
No literacy, only the wide screen's flat
Emptiness consoled them as they grew.
The white van grows old in darkening blue.

Now London riots, Birmingham's on fire.
Young looters grab and smash their souls' desire,
Police must stand and watch while violence
Murders a peaceful man, and a woman leaps
From the second floor to desperate safety through
Mocking flames and swelling smoke in Croydon's
Broken village. Alone, a child sleeps
In the shadow of a falling tower, orphan of gardens,
On a concrete field where singing finches flew.
The black, the white, the golden, all minds grey,
Sent fatherless and creedless out to prey.

Why does this cause me grief? I grew up there,
My first long years, and breathed fog-laden air,
Thick fog that fell and blinded. When it passed,
Suburban houses shone, their roses green.
Haughty, majestic swans glided on the lake,
Fought over soaked stale bread, stalked along grassed,
Gentle parkland. Paths and hooped fences lay between
Wooded slopes. You might have thought it would last,
That civilisation drowsing, half-awake
In the afternoon, while death grew in its heart.
A child walked home in the evening, safe, apart.

What history brings, and what it floods away,
Ten thousand spirits starving in broad day,
Tens of thousands, maybe millions, free
From love and faith and hope. These fall
Like murder on our streets. And every one
Unique and irreplaceable as the tree
Crashing before the bulldozer, its tall
And pale trunk, its flowers of liberty
Tearing, plummeting, crackling in the sun.
Sweet souls rise, parch and fail year by year.
Fools turn aside, and this can happen here.

Wellington Square

What natural thoughts, what yearning
Brought these two to this bitter pass?
They sit on the damp grass
The shifting shadows fleck,
And all around, the city's gleams,
Its living souls flow by in streams
Of sparkling eyes intent on trade or learning,
Sex, promotion, fear,
Eddying past the wide, leafy park, near
And infinitely remote from the patch of faint
Light where they sit, a can of paint
Swaying from each young neck.

What are these wounded souls, and whom
Should you pity more – these two
Beleaguered in clouds of paint and glue
Or that bureaucrat in his tower,
Beleaguering each hour,
Pursuing his career at the expense
Of compassion, knowledge, entrance
To the park where children flounder in the fume
That rises from abuse, indifference,
And withers into leaves, pollen, sky?
Speak no more of the futile. Pass him by.

The Conference

It's like a nightmare you know you're having
and can't quite wake from. The nascent sun
grows patiently towards the noonday strength
it will use to parch the summer-scalded leaves
and cook the roads. I want to get to the city.
The traffic clogs my way like choking veins.

The conference brims. It settles and drifts
with professionals eager to know. A keynote
speaker illuminates thought and screen
with summations of misery. Eight million
souls, he tells us, breathe in the sorrowing
world's expanse of prisons. An encrustation

of hurt and harm that grows
as death spreads over fields long neglected,
crops turned to stone. Thomas Aquinas
wrote and dictated eight million words
in his years of labour and prayer. For every one
a prisoner chafes against alien walls.

Up the stairs and into a narrow room
to hear the language of pain and wisdom,
science and faith. My conference kit
rests on a chair beside me. John Cassian
interviewed monks to study
lives of contemplation and love

for Christ who died, thirsting for water
and souls. These, our researchers,
talked with prisoners in stifling cities,
learned how captives long to live clean
of the drug that led them to their cages.
Despair, wrote Thomas Nashe,

is never complete till it kills its victim
and so itself. This cancer of the young
swells to a black crescendo in empty places,
cells and toilet blocks and bedrooms,
fears the touch of a voice. A glance
of patience, a mind that listens. Who can share

the morning with those who have travelled into night?
Nashe reminds me: A stay in prison
is part of a gentleman's education. And Jesus: I was sick and in
  prison
and you visited. Judges sentence
less cruelly than the world. Our innocent torturers
smile and do not forgive us.

And now it's over. The glass doors open
on road, car park, harbour, and hot sky. But the murder
of Christ enacts itself daily in tavern and car,
cell block and bare apartment. My God, my God, why
have you forsaken me? Torn faces
shelter from the sun outside the methadone clinic.

Letter to a Judge

Spring, Your Honour, starts to warm the plane trees.
Mirrors of rainfall still dampen the road.
I've lived another winter under my load
Of guilt, poverty, remorse and tears that freeze
In the cold gusts as I shed them. My robberies weigh
Heavily on my heart. The cathedral stands
Crowning its hill with faith and foreign lands'
Languages and worshippers. I stray
Footsore among walls of glittering grey,
Garish windows, shoppers' long unease.

Tomorrow I shall meet you again. My sentence looms
Unfinished in your thought. Movies of violence
Given and suffered play colourfully on my conscience,
Scars and band-aids, hours waiting in courtrooms.
I've tried to keep the terms of my parole.
A theft, some drug arrests, a handful of fights.
I've followed a stream of blood through houseless nights.
I walk and remember by the road where the great wheels roll.
Day by day, in the broken land of my soul,
From unseen roots the rose of forgiveness blooms.

I'd like to face the summer free from all
The shadows of the light, steel bands of mind,
If you, Your Honour, think good to be kind
And grant me absolution from the tall
Towers of earth that grow and menace me.
Next week, next year, other prisoners will plead.
I wish you well, judging their bitter need
When I am long forgotten, and the city
Wakes to spring and pollen yet to be,
Green parrots chatter and dash, and magpies call.

II

Cemetery Beach

Near Cemetery Beach the church lies drowned
On a sandy bed, past tide, past shoal
And shark, and schools of fish swerve round
Cold rock and seaweed, sands that roll
On depths of sea, refracting sound
And bending light. The steeple burns
  In the hidden sun, luminous fathoms below
  The waves, the coast where heavy vessels flow
  Gracefully north. The current ebbs and turns.

Squid worship in the chancel. Eels
Dance around pillars. Perch pray
Then rise and shimmer through the aisles,
Green kelp sails and minnows play.
And stained glass in the light reveals
Its ancient scenes of loss and grace
  To show a house beyond the changing tide,
  The violence of the ocean's spears, blank pride
  Of hungry eyes. A dhufish lifts its face

Towards the altar wreathed in green.
Sand falls through long discarded nets.
Stinging jellyfish drift between
The nave and rail. The sky forgets
The church beneath the waves, unseen
And unremembered. Shadows fight
  And drink in shaded bars. Day wakes dead air.
  It dwindles on the hot parades. Under water's glare,
  Oysters confess their faith in the secret light.

On an epitaph in the Nicholson Museum

Child, your little life was ended,
Bounded by an hour of wrongness,
Long before your body reached its
Destined form. Your nurse who caused these

Words in stone remembered. Sisters,
Mother, father, brothers, neighbours,
Friends, oblivion caught them, ages
Keep them in their dark tomorrows.

Six millennia surround you,
Jug, papyrus fragment, family
Letter, past oneiromancy,
Vase, amphora, mace-heads, mummy

Wound in cerements forever,
Endless living, endless dying,
Sleep in death, await returning
Silence with each evening's twilight.

Alexander's general, Ptolemy,
Watches from unseeing eyelids
Hermes, Dionysus dream you.
Ibis-head Osiris guards you.

After Horace, Ode 1.11

Leave numerology
To strangers in health food stores; you can't know
What sort of end is given
To you or me, only that it is; better to endure
Whatever the season; whether he's giving us
One winter of many, when the white rocks
Above the beach wear down the rain,
Or our last; be thoughtful, taste
Fresh grapes, don't let hope in its cramped hours
Ramble unpruned.
                While you read this,
Crops are dying, never to flower again.
Tomorrow's no more real
Than last year's promises; harvest the day.

Mermaid

Native half to the sea and half to land,
Fearful that someone may glimpse her, she rests on the shore,
Warming her human flesh, a shell in one hand,
Ridged and whorled like her delicate ear. Scales pour,
Green, blue, pink-flecked, glistening in the day,
From hips to fins. She tosses her hair back, slides
Awkwardly across the sand down into the grey,
Windy, white-capped ocean. There she hides

With the cold, sharp coral, striped fish that dart
Suddenly in shafts of weaving light, or gleams
Of sea snakes, fronds of seaweed reaching, playing
Endlessly from their long banks. Now her heart,
Released from land's weariness, leaps in the streams,
Hunts with the hammerhead shark, the black ray straying.

The Heron and the Moon

Whose waves, whose rocks, whose flecked spume rising
From foaming, rushing reefs, whose tangled scrubland
Sloping up to twilit hills? Whose white moon sliding
Out of ancient, ephemeral clouds; lone, dark stand
Of troubled trees against the broken sky,
Grey beach where lovers and a murderer once ran
Under eternal cold years? A heron's cry
Peals against sea's long rumble.
                            But who am I,
Standing by a steel fence post, transient as the crow
That vanishes above the cliff, shadow of a man –
His life crammed into a canvas backpack, no
Home, no world, no reason, while the sand
Counts time – to hold the stony waves in my hand,
The heron and the moon, then let them go?

Performance Poem

Maybe, you think, the conductor's drunk.
The horns are riddled with hiccups.
Is this improvisation? Are we playing to a score?
Staves are smudged and tattered,
Pages have blown into the alley. Or it's free jazz,
Unbound by repressive logic of chords and octaves,
Urban clangour shattering cool woodwinds.
So you think. You play through time
Like a symphony flowing in and out of silence,
Only you can't hear it,
Or only in fitful echoes between traffic noises.
Sometimes those pure harmonies, rising to sweet crescendos,
Sound still from a bedroom long ago,
Fracturing discords among sleepless dawn's bereavements.

Black Dog

Black dog, black mongrel, the bitch that bore you
Should have been strangled in a gutter.

Misbegotten under a poisoned trunk,
Sacred to all manner of dark gods,

Weaned on toe of newt – No,
Come here, puppy, your family tree's entwined

With mine. You paw through my album, goaded
By who knows what well-meaning friends,

Parents of friends, heedless colleagues.
You slaver near gates of unreason, where measured voices preach

Against truth, worship, song. Leave me, puppy,
Let me dance to the music that gave

The lion and the timid lynx respite,
And turned the hunter's thoughts to listening and prayer.

The oldest woods

The oldest woods are new, need not have been.
The ancient karri, boughs gracing troubled
Century after century, lest the chainsaw come,
Orchid, kangaroo paw, scurrying soil,

Cloud the karri climbs toward and sighs.
Its restless tossing brushes empty air,
Floods the valley with parti-coloured song.
Towns with hills and aerials push against forest.

They stretch out hands toward waking fields. All things,
Being new, and drawn from deep, unfathomed wells
Of what may be, may not be, rise as gifts

Standing against the word that grants them room
To spread and flower, welcome nesting birds,
Record eternal truth in a grey trunk.

A Confession for Duns Scotus

1

Parade to the drum beat of the age?
Once – having trained in my youth
In the seventies' boot camps – once I would have said so.
A nineteen sixty-two Holden,
Canary yellow, but rusted, exuding song
And suntan lotion, rocks and rumbles
Toward the beach. The water
Burns toward heaven. About which –
Four decades in the past –
I know nothing.
      I know nothing.
Three decades in the past. There is no God,
I said (the fool!) with my mouth. Waves of social progress
Founder on rocks of reality.
Children drown in the foam.
Platoons of the half-educated
Prowl under moth-flown lamps,
Kick holes in the lifeboats.

But the light of God caresses
The mountainous summits of tinglewood
Rain blesses and wind wounds
Under icy constellations
Torn by clouds.

2

You were the eagle of the north.
In Oxford, Paris, Cologne,
You studied to frame the sun.
You saw further, more cleanly.
Your logic touched the moment's
Living pulse with love.

Philosophy so precise
It lived in theology's mirror.
Eye for the body's grace,
Lips faithful in movement.
Hope in the violent seas,
Truth and truth unfolding.

3

      Well,
I was given something.
Not for any wisdom, courage, fire,
Certainly not accomplishment.

Waiting patiently beside the river,
Subtlety born from wisdom, wisdom raised in faith,
A young theologian from the border country.

He points to an overhanging branch,
One among hundreds. Golden liquidambar.
Its leaves gather time.

The Fallen Tree

A playful, twining footpath, sharp with ferns
And golden bracken's fire, peace that burns
And air that soothes. Hard greenery freshly woken
From summer sleep. Over the stony way,
And down the valley, crushing leaf and clay,
A grey prince among karri trees lies broken,
Clusters of leaves tumbled in death. A thick
Trunk fell ruined into huge fragments,
Round, uneven, rough, random monuments
To random wind. Sheared away like a matchstick,
Long splinters jab at unrepentant day
From a newly shredded stump. Now it will stand
Alone and maimed, a warning to the land
That winds destroy, till it moulders into sand.

III

What is beyond the stars

And sometimes what is beyond the stars appears,
Though fitfully, you might easily miss it –
Stained glass in the sanctuary of an old church,
A crown upheld in the silence.

An infant's hand unfurling, discovering fingers.
Grey ibis in formation over scrubland.
They draw the king's banners behind them
In the remote air, you can read the words

If you see past the traffic, the semi-trailers
Queued on the highway, the low, arcane trees
Alive with scarlet flowers and secret wings.

The words say: Blessed are those who mourn.
And: Sometimes what is beyond the stars
Appears, and sacred ibis draw their banners.

Portrait of an Old Man

A portrait hangs at the end of a long hall
In the labyrinthine art gallery, near
The still, grey city. Yellow stars fall
Into smoke and cloud. Now, while the room is clear
Of students, visitors, cleaners, the old man's eyes
Twinkle in his canvas. Painted midnight skies
And dark fir-trees surround him, and a distant rise
Of another city's towers, granite, tall,
Reaching the gilded frame. His ancient cheeks
Are red, pitted with silver. The portrait speaks.

And when the gallery opens, first a young
Teacher arrives, a guidebook in her palm,
And sees, gathered in the foreground, among
Towers, trees and distant white clouds, calm
Children staring up at the waking light
Where lately an old man smiled. Her laughing sight
Traces their hands. They learn the world's delight,
Ephemeral on canvas, framed and hung
On a grey wall, and rich with layered paint.
Her attention drifts. The children's forms grow faint.

The teacher leaves. The white-haired face returns
To its tranquil, landscaped scene. And now a man,
Pale features lined, strolls in. His blue squint burns,
He studies well, as critically as he can,
Awakening pornography and sexual sweat,
Flesh to remember, faces to forget,
Assesses it for realism, and yet
He knows he stains the love his mockery spurns
With every moment pondering those white
And starlit bodies groaning in the night.

Two artists nod at the painting, smile and sigh.
One finds a riddle coded in the trees,
The other discerns a cold, eternal sky,
A winter sun, wild eagles, broken seas.
A lonely child meets herself and grins.
In a blue summer playground where life begins,
Painted, gathered families, men's and women's
Mouths and hands applaud and prophesy
While the wind blows. She tracks her mother's wise
Intensity, compassion and deep eyes.

The aged man smiles down from his neutral wall.
He watches the past, the future and the ending
Day, turbulence of strangers passing, all
Vivid in the gallery's brilliance, blending
Into old and new paintings. Each has his own
Colours, textures, composition, tone,
Each caught in a different frame, alone
For a moment in a portrait or in small,
Receding landscapes, the haunted, transient shows.
The gallery closes. The old man's portrait glows.

The Tiger in the Vineyard

Heavy, hanging vine leaves wrap and enfold
Wire, trellis and gnarled brown wood the morning
Darkens with its light. Misted, dusty, ripening
Green grapes spread, and the sun dances its cold,
Changing, ephemeral path where the tiger strayed,
Its fierce glance vigilant, its graceful paws
Lightly treading the earth between rows. Harsh claws
Stretch and score the ground. Tremulous shade

Echoes the steps of the sun and the predator's rise.
Deep yellow, angry dark gold and a sudden
Whiteness glint from its fur. Rough shadows leap
Where it springs in passionate joy, then lies to sleep
In a narrow lane of sand, all but hidden
Among rich vines. Leaves play on its flickering eyes.

Murderer and Child

Three nights ago father was violent again. Today
He plays outside in the warm sun with his boy.
Three nights ago shouts and cracks, the fist's sway
Broke twilight to tears. No child's toy
Could help with this. Mother tightened her hand,
Pled a headache, didn't understand
Their son's trembling agony, or the shades
That scoured his father. Tomorrow he will fly
Alone across the Pacific. Today death fades
Into the grass and they laugh at the hot sky.

With thirteen murders on his soul, he swings
His four-year-old on his shoulder. Sun's
Music plays through ficus leaves and brings
Harmony to the green roses. He runs,
Carrying his boy, across the lawn to where
Two stumps of vanished trees wait, grey and bare.
On Glebe Point Road the buses squeal and groan.
Looking up at the house violence
Bought, he sits on a tree-trunk like a throne,
And stares across the bloodshed into silence.

Sweet coral atolls, impossibly white,
Sewn with forest, caught in wreaths of blue,
Capture dawn below him. And he takes his flight
Eastward into morning. Then the plane drops through
Tangles of smog to a roaring American town.
For nights and hours he marks his target down,
Inconsequently strolls behind him. Blood-defiled
Pavement spreads in weltering day.
Dead limbs reach toward the traffic. Child,
You wouldn't know your father now, as he walks away.

Another plane eases west, descends. The cabin dark,
Lights string jewels around the black void,
Sing over empty buildings. Street, bridge, park,
Factory and warehouse, car yard, destroyed
Terraces pass by as he drives alone
Homeward. Then the towering wells of his own
Country. Churches and bookshops on Glebe Point Road.
Ruler in exile of an anguished place,
He turns the key. He sits, lets fall his load,
Climbs the stairs, and touches his child's face.

Museum of Contemporary Art

Through the smoky streets of a sullen town
Dumb with noise, violent with sudden colours,
Reds and golds from trees offering flowers
To an uncomprehending morning, dull and brown
As loudspeakers blaring in stations. Then up the broad
   Steps the sun touches with streams
Vanishing in the dust. We push through revolving doors,
Buy tickets and enter a warrior's hall of dreams,
   Hung with weapons, battle-axe, sword,
Machete, flamethrower, centuries of wars.

Machine-guns' intricate workings, arrows' pride,
Dart and slingshot, missiles of deadly time,
Line the route to the first floor. We climb
The welcoming stairs, and galleries open wide
Their vistas of modernity. In a white,
   Imageless emptiness, painted tiles
Form the margin. Random signs in free
Calligraphy stain them. A choppy coast and miles
   Of grey sand sleep opposite. Light
Sparks from the waves. Fishing boats pull out to sea.

Youthful sunbathers, tumbled, rocky hills,
Bring their painted life to a pale shore.
A collection of farmhouses, fields, harvest's store
Ripening in desolate barns and gold frames fills
A long, quiet room. Women at market stalls
   Buy painted apples, cherries, pears
From deep wicker baskets. A butcher sells
Skinned and gutted red-streaked rabbits, hares.
   Golden evening sunlight falls
On darkening stone churches, polished bells.

In the next gallery, a massive battle scene
Towers to the ceiling. Forgotten soldiers die
Clutching at nothing. Small bombers fly
Into seas of cloud. Bodies in jungle green
Gape in front of a shattered village. Guns
   Burn like jewels in soft dark.
Black shells of schoolhouses and farms
Dance in their smoke. Alive with leaf and bark,
   An innocent, rippling river runs.
Prisoners in narrow cells raise thin, chained arms.

Rusted wire sculptures taunt the corridor
With shapes of disintegration. A woman stands,
Naked, eternal, melodic. Her onyx hands,
Open palms, extended fingers, pour
Cold light. A thirteenth century cathedral,
   Ripe with echoes of golden fire,
Chants from stained glass windows a calm, slow
Hymn to silence. Gargoyle frowning, spire
   Reaching into music, tall
And subtle, touch the shadows with their glow.

Living trees extend through a shaded hall.
Their branches, feathered with dense green, explore
Windowsill and cornice. The carpeted floor
Creaks, buckles, breaks where thick roots crawl.
Brilliant red flowers perfume the air.
   A black and white movie plays
To a tiny room. Flickering mouths and eyes
Re-enact a memory of pointless days
   In a European landscape where
Bomb craters crumble under black and white skies.

At the end of the last cool gallery, colours show
Explosions of gunfire in the corner of a high canvas.
Farmers take their trucks to market, pass
Gentle houses in crisp morning. Below,
A forest spreads its tendrils around the frame,
   Filigreed silver and green fern.
A summer sun warms naked swimmers, meets
Two children waiting in white before a lectern.
   They shelter candles' low flame.
Smouldering rifles lead us back to the streets.

The Painter

She works on a large canvas. Children in their crowds
Ebb and mill around her. The harbour shines
Through the gallery's broad windows. Light-flecked clouds
Pass across morning while her hand places lines,
   Colours and shades.
She traces a wide cross, detailed with designs,
The city's moments, cruciform parades.

The cross extends its open arms. She paints
On the left, among well-dressed family and friends, a couple,
A young woman and man under the eyes of saints
In stained glass, bridesmaids and groomsmen. A circle,
   Gold and white,
Closes the scene, and she makes light dwindle
So that the wedding shifts between day and night.

Wild birds decorate the upright,
Eagle, ibis, hawk, seagull and osprey,
Whirled and gathered, twined in the delight
Of living mastery of air and day.
   Feathered wings
Rise against the unseen wind and play
Silent sonatas, and the canvas sings.

In the centre a flowery triangle frames a view
Of homeless teenagers sleeping in a ute
That won't drive anywhere again. Dark rain drips through
A broken windscreen. Mists pollute
   The grassy ground.
A stand of trees. White roses. Bamboos shoot
Into the grey-lit fog. The young sleep sound.

On the right arm she shapes a glimpse of crime.
Five bitter figures kicking one who lies
Curled on the roadway. Puddles of star-flecked calm
Darken the bitumen. Hate fills their eyes.
  Dull boots thud
To skull, to chest, temples, groin and thighs.
Images of seraphim wake to flood

The painted sky with praise. Vistas of rain
Appear to left and right, patches of air,
Angels peering over them, fields of grain
In miniature, and lit skyscrapers where
  The breaking town
Patterns the canvas with its tumult. There
She signs her name, and throws her brushes down.

The Hanged Man

Ripples gleam and slap, and evening thickens
Over the wide harbour. Riddling hills
Gather, and the horizon falls and darkens.
The trivial, variegated song of frivolity spills
In a splatter of light from the restaurant on the pier,
Its broad windows golden. A white yacht
Sways at its mooring. On a pillar here
At the bitumen's edge, a plaque confesses what
The convict settlement suffered – fathers, brothers,
Sons mouldering on gibbets, a warning to others.

Far from home, I shiver beside the sea,
And seem to watch a prisoner who met his death
Long ago at the gallows' cruelty
Hovering over the water, voice without breath,
Form without substance. His shadow claims the land
And the chopping waves, and he speaks without sound
Trouble of forgotten years. The gibbets stand
Unseen and harsh, condemning the peaceful ground.
Silent fires of twilight echo shame's
Indifference, and hidden history flames.

He saw the morning the last convict ship,
Long after they hanged him, arrived with its freight of grief.
He heard the last prisoners' voices slip
Into oblivion, murderer, blackmailer, thief.
Years later he heard eager recruits
In uniform, answering the call
Of distant war, the crunch and thump of boots,
Rifles drumming. He knew which men must fall
On beaches and in trenches far away,
Who must return scarred to endure the day.

Governments fall and oppositions rise.
He sees cabinets meeting in their boardrooms.
Children run and squeal where tragedy lies
Buried under the foreshore, the seagulls' tombs,
Fishes' graves between the tides and grass.
Picnic places in the sunlight, trust that lives,
Mothers cutting sandwiches while memories pass
Into emptiness and music that forgives.
He watches the rainbow breaking over the sea,
The transient light that sets the prisoner free.

Music blasts like warfare from the restaurant,
A loud door opening. The lost man's gaze
Drifts towards the pier, noise that can't
Evade the coming days, and won't erase
Children shuddering in cold rooms through nights of dread.
The city spreads, bustling towards the sky.
He knows the light, the strangers and the dead
Mourning their wasted hours. White gulls fly
Above the shore, the falling, deep grey coasts.
Rocks arouse cold waves to a sea of ghosts.

I pace alone around the starry bay.
Ripples run and eddy, rustle and fight.
I puzzle what this dead man has to say
To me, flown from the west across fading light.
I have my own ghosts that follow me,
Their silence beats my ear like a drum
Pounding the air above the trembling sea,
Songs of loss and agony to come.
Countless living souls surround me, torn
By ecstasy and sadness still unborn.

Maybe he remembers a small house in England,
A lover and their daughters, and the poor
Comfort taken from him. He knows each hand
Lifted in violence, love shattered on the floor,
Despairing children's terror, and where calm
Builds homes, and generations grow and learn.
Couples walk the pier, arm in arm.
Soundless questions fill the night and burn
Truth into my heart. The hanged man's soul
Cries out across the sea, and small waves roll.

The Funeral Ship

1

Death rides the ocean like a summit of burning
Black cloud that lines the long horizon
Or a surfer paddling out to sea, golden
In the darkening sun, or a cold ship returning
From travels to sordid harbours. History
Haunts the dunes with its murderous galleries
Past, present and to come; and my own small agonies
Loom out of the scrub like wraiths of misery.
High above the beach the church of St John
The Divine bodies white fire of revelation.

A lifetime's travel behind me, the silent sand
Calls me with its mystery. Monuments of seaweed
Huddle against incoming night. Shadows bleed
From damp rocks. I cup the sea in my hand,
Run the surf through my fingers. My hired car
Stands on the road above me, loaded with dust.
The sun settles into the waves like rust,
Like memories dying under a chilly star.
Imagination draws me back through centuries
Of trouble and fire to another coast, fresh seas.

2

Innocent of feather-spattering oil,
Untrammelled by technology's glare and roar,
The sea caresses a sixth century shore.
Gulls curvet whitely above the spoil
Of uncivil war. White and black, they screech,
Wail and plummet, their beaks open, bold
And angry. The waves' endlessness, cold,
Tipped with blood and foam, claws the beach
Where a man lies dying, surrounded by the shades
Of his fallen conscript army, and his breathing fades.

A long, low boat sways in the death-stained sea,
Waits in the shallows. A woman dressed in red,
Another in blue and green, wade past the dead
To the dying man. They lift him reverently.
Crunching over seashells with cautious feet,
They carry him to the craft and lay him there,
Pebbles under their steps, salt in their hair.
They cast off, and oars plunge and beat.
The few mourners watch the ship recede,
While all around them wounded soldiers bleed.

A thousand years pass. The boat survives tornadoes,
Rainstorms blackening the sea, days of sunlight
Burning on a slow, green swell. Cavernous, white
Icebergs drift from the north. It glides under rainbows.
It passes explorers risking lives to know,
Unwashed pirates grinning at cruel rapes,
Passengers drowning in fierce, fathomless seascapes.
The pall-bearers? Vanished now. But the years' tides flow,
The boat carries its bones, its music sings,
Meteors fall, and cormorants beat their wings.

It floats untroubled under bombing raids
On blacked-out harbour cities dressed to die.
Battleships' drumming guns deafen the sky.
It makes its way through sea mines, naval blockades.
Submariners observe it as they drown.
Coral reefs emerge to break the waves
From ruined decks and hidden, rusting graves.
Torpedoed warships, hundreds of fathoms down,
Welcome strange and secret fishes' ways.
The boat endures hot nights and crimson days.

Dirk Hartog crosses its wake, and William Dampier,
Charting what will become Australia's bays.
White strands, deep trees, and where the sun sways
Above an unmapped river, a single spear
Whistles in the steep air. New pirates fight
From the maimed hills and violent coasts of Somalia,
Terrorise crew and travellers, oil tanker,
Slow cargo vessel. The boat moves, light
And lifted by the waves, past wars and mountains,
Pleasure cruises, the seven fiery oceans.

Civilisations falter, and escapees
From broken cities and families camp in cars,
Sleep on the beach under featureless, friendless stars.
The boat rocks on gently swelling seas,
Patches of brown sand and dark weed swirling.
Storms rumble, shipwrecks wake and pass.
Patient, emotionless, sharks cruise through sea grass.
Waves devour fishers, and church bells ring
To summon congregations to the word
Unspoken, bread untasted, hymns unheard.

3

The sky mounts above the sea like flame.
The grey scrub before my tears grows black.
A plant struggles beside the sandy track
That meets the road. It clings to life like a name
To a spirit in the tumult of the waves, a call
Alone and desperate in the growing night to be heard,
To be recognised as the world sinks like a bird
Under the howling wind. The waves tremble and fall.
I remember the shame and treachery of my days,
A dream of rebirth, salt air, a breath of praise.

The funeral ship rises in the morning
To the sea's fruits. Its decks shine with gifts
Of decorated quilts, and the tide lifts
Fish on board with wreaths of seaweed. Wailing
Gulls bring toys and flowers, and new thoughts live.
Where the dead man crumbled, a baby lies
Blinking up at the sun with new, round eyes.
Dolphins and mermaids attend him. Eagles give
Shelter, and sea nymphs feed him from their breasts.
Whales chant lullabies. The child rests.

The Sea Gods

Winter clouds mounted over the sea and tore
Waves with curving gusts of broken weather,
Waves that swelled and ran and crashed together
Loudly, coldly, dragged stony sand from the shore.
I watched from my seventh floor window, safe and warm.
Cold light spread like ice under the storm, and three
Strange, majestic figures grew out of the sea,
Moving slowly. Cloud and foam took form,

The trees shivered. Were they embodied dreams,
Visions of past frustrations and deaths contending
For mastery over the winter tides? Long rain
Veiled their fingers' movements, their faces' gleams,
Tidal gestures and streaming arms blending
Into water, three shields, two swords, a centaur's mane.

Shopping for Clothes

'You look sensational in tears, loss and silence.'
The sales assistant helps arrange long days
In solitary mourning, shadows of patience,
Around her shoulders. In the mall a busker plays
Hollow notes on a hand-carved wooden flute
To the patter of an African drum.
Shoppers in slow tides come
Drifting through the open doors to gaze
On ranged identities, blouse and skirt and suit.

They fumble in the racks, throng sale stands.
'Here's a sweet gown in death.' She lowers it on.
Ribbons of red pour down her arms and hands.
Deep wounds mark her sides with woven crimson,
Children's blood, the blood of naked strangers.
A finger-tapped rhythm calls
From canvas market stalls.
She views the scars that shape her flesh, the fallen
Gathered around her, young soldiers, travellers.

'Or you could dress in loveliness like gold petals
Among labyrinths of greenery as daylight grows,
Marsupials hurry into nests and mist settles,
Or dawn touching a fiery wave as it flows
To scatter into foam on a shore with white trees,
Black, savage rocks that blossom.
This is our shelf of wisdom,
Green sadness, threads of compassion the strong robe shows,
Colours that move like music to the hum of bees.'

In the window hangs a kimono of fine, white silk,
Painted with maroon dragons that tremble and shake
When the air shifts. Cold like snow, like milk
On a far mountain morning, its perfections ache
Through the bloodstained beauty of the merchandise,
Dark orchids, destiny's war.
By night the dragons soar
Above the city, into the starlight, wake
The sleeping sun with scarlet wings of ice.

The Stripper

In the back room at a city hotel, she strips
To entertain an amateur football team.
Chairs stacked in shadow against the far wall seem
Watchers behind the watchers. Her costume slips
From shoulders, thighs. Outside is a pavement, then
A universe waiting to engulf the awkward men
Whose forced sophistication bleeds and aches,
Tumbles into rough laughter when the music breaks.

She has her life, though they scoff and call her trash.
The rhythm clatters and pulses through a thin
And starveling sound system, and her hands begin
What she hopes are inviting gestures, clumsy, slapdash
Figures of loneliness. As invisible
To the ringing faces around her as an angel
Hovering over an office block of black light,
Her thought conceals its flame. She caresses the night.

How many strippers can dance on the point of a needle?
How many angels on a tawdry hotel floor?
The song crackles and ends, and becomes no more
Than a fragment of age-long silences that dwindle
To the cold roar of the starlit ocean. She preserves
Her solitude, dresses and leaves. No one observes
The music behind her eyes, the melody
Growing and burning, the night sea's agony.

Departure Lounge

How often have we travelled from the shriek
Of seagulls on the western shore
To the green mountains? Over the engine's roar,
We sample anecdotes from a troubled store
Of reminiscence. Now and then we speak
Uncertainly about our chance
To touch the ground before the dance
Sinks to its destined end. Compassionate prayer
Plays in the quiet places of the mind,
Touches our losses, all we leave behind,
The gull's lonely cry, the coasts we share.

The intensive care unit dreams and hums.
(Gulls quarrel on a sunlit beach,
Lift angry wings and peck at scraps.) Now each
Breath seems an accomplishment. Monitors teach
The rhythms of mortality. The surgeon comes,
Draws measured words of hope from dread.
My thoughts glance from bed to bed,
And four patients drowse, waiting, apart,
Alone, for the laughing messenger to arrive,
Or a gentle voice to call one to survive
The ill-treated spirit, the injured heart.

Here on the third floor is the centre of the earth,
Elliptical, broken from the rest.
Hanging wires link monitor and chest.
Bleak mechanisms pattern heartbeats, test
The body's strength to live, the treatment's worth.
(A pelican glides across a dark lake.
The wind whistles. Grey trees shake.)
Our friend lives. We talk with him. He sleeps.
Here is the centre of the world. Hours flow
Outward to the roses, return here to show
The truth of days, the trembling moment's deeps.

One man lived. Three drowsing patients died.
Flames shimmer on the water's face.
Mourners bend and keen in a far-off place
Where seagulls mount and soar. A sigh of grace,
Pulse of an instant not to be denied.
Again the chance to walk and learn.
Eagles swoop and rivers burn
Under calm, impartial hills that welcome him home.
You are the gardener who plants apple in our land,
Sculpts the wings of fire. I clasp your hand.
We fly over city and forest, and white sea's foam.

A Fallen Soldier

Green, turbulent hills, and jacaranda,
Mauve, green, playing in the spring's warm wind
Like rippling, dancing banners of miniature nations
Where peace flowered and families sang. Orchards,
Apple, pear, cherry, soft blossoms and crisp,
Sunlit leaves in their ranks. Then ospreys, parade-ground
And my camp bed near the battlefield. Bloodstained
Teenage boys gasping in their khaki. Tufted
Hillocks and the sea shuddering.

You think the old are patient. So I am,
When my grandchildren visit and the world's new
Laughter rises above magpies' talk, or a golden
Sun of contentment glows on fearful waves,
Seaweed waltzing. But when children sleep
In cars and there's no nourishment, when crystal meth
Explodes and sudden rage burns and murders,
A child reaches for a mother who's flown away,
Then I'm no longer tranquil.

I hurry through arcades and see patterns of desperation
Cover sterile walls. Then I turn to the streets
And rape blackens the night and claws at the future.
Righteous crowds clatter into the darkness,
Away from their children bleeding. The wars we fought,
The leaping, implacable sea, white freesias,
Warm flesh collapsing into evening clouds,
Cockatoos' anger. Vines rain from dry trees.
Dead battles of the dead.

A feather fallen from the wing of time. Neither
You that write my words nor those that listen
Know the lost music that breaks like lightning
On my mind's ear, dove's beckoning, drums of long ago.
Abstractions drove us to kill, bleed and sweat
And know the shock of wounds, thoughts like freedom,
Passions like love, memories of orchards,
My mother's teacups on their yellow hooks in the kitchen,
Dogwood roses in the sun.

An Emptiness of Rivers

I tried to build a heaven but I failed.
The windows and the doors were shaped from flame,
Cold, curved blades of fire arranged to frame
Walls of white cloud, floors of sunrise, nailed
By lightning. Its tiles were violet evening, turned
Over joists and gutters of grey morning. But an emptiness
Of sand-flecked rivers washed the gates with blankness,
Brought down drizzle where the lintels had burned,

Quenched the sky. Now (since you've helped) from the past's
Embers a house of word and image, sown
With dark-petalled green garden silence has grown.
Black vines flower on its shelves. It lasts
Through autumn equinox, winter solstice, then summer
Searing the grass, hot nights, fig tree's whisper.

The Silver Cylinder

I wrote this poem on a tiny scrap of parchment
In miniature calligraphy and sealed it
In a silver cylinder on the left leg of a stint,
And set it free with its companions to hop and flit
And chirrup before they rise to migrate together
Across ocean, city, reef and continent
To settle beside some distant lake in the shelter
Of friendly reeds. Maybe an ornithologist
Will find it, decipher these strange foreign words,
Or, parted from its fragile cloud of birds,
The stint will meet its end in a leaping forest
Of dark fir under a predator's claws
And hot eyes, and the cylinder will be lost
Among mouldering, fallen bark and wet bracken.
Or it will pass through the fire of a cold shark's jaws
And drift on its tiny limb of white bone, tossed
And drowned by the tides, into wells of thoughtless ocean.

The Northbridge Sculptures

Graceful in granite, they stand outside the café.
People wander by. Some pause to stare,
Some wince and smile, and turn their thoughts away.
A young woman, her round shoulders bare,
  Larger than life, her hair flowing,
  Waving, motionless but glowing,
Bows her head to sniff a can of paint.
In her left arm a granite baby feeds
From a granite bottle. Her bent gaze recedes
From the tables into the clouds of fool or saint.
Her sculpted hair ripples and burns like day.

I cross the narrow, sunlit road to see
Marble figures carved in high relief
On a nightclub wall. Revealed delicately,
Vines wander, and under falling leaf
  And opening flower, three young
  Children sprawl, drunk, among
Bottles and needles. Mouths gape wide,
Arms flung anyhow, poised in stone,
Ragged clothes torn carelessly, shoes thrown
On cold white grass. Caught with a sculptor's pride,
Their fixed marble eyes weep hopelessly.

Their hands arch. Fingers curl towards the vines
Wreathed and clinging over a panelled frieze.
A sculpted golden house, its breathing lines
Clean with Hellenic symmetry, oak trees,
   Carved in gold where drifters pass,
   Anchoring its emerald grass,
Overshadows a car park. Its rooms protect
A bruised and hungry child on his bed,
A man's fist rising, a shouting head,
An old, blind woman dying of neglect.
Oak branches shade gold soil. The garden shines.

Three silver wolves leap at the adult store.
Two alabaster bureaucrats, thick files
Under suited arms, pass stonily by, ignore
The suffering children, look aside, their smiles
   Figuring their slow thoughts' chill,
   Empty eyes and useless will.
Near them, prison bars, arranged in wood
Alongside the windows of an old hotel,
Frame a woman's arms stretching from hell
To the lost heaven of her daughters who sit and brood
On the deadly street, doves on a firelit shore.

Across the traffic lights. And now a scene
Of marble violence. Two bikies swing
Broken pool cues, stride in rage between
Three fallen, bloodied enemies, who wring
   Fractured hands imploring calm.
   Polished muscles on each arm
Are shaped and wrought with strong Homeric grace.
White marble gleams from noses, foreheads, chins,
Grimaces of the conquered, victors' grins,
Vacancy of each twenty-first century face,
Bitter tragedy of the small and mean.

And finally, before the library,
Three philosophers pursue their long debate,
Granite fingers joined in harmony.
Grecian, bearded, one holds out a slate
   Carved with the terrible, hackneyed word
   Travellers to Delphi heard:
Know yourself. Another bears a page
Carrying the thought: Know nature. One defends
This text: Know people, family, strangers, friends,
Passion and shame, the savagery of the age.
A wordless figure, framed behind the three,

Clothed elegantly in marbled satin veins,
Points at heaven, or nothing, or the sky.
Music pours from rhythmic hair, contains
The sculptures, buildings, steps, the passers-by
  In a marble gesture. Music drops
  On nightclubs, banks and coffee shops.
The city's noises break and part like waves
On frozen, sculpted shores that never change,
Like iron currents flowing out of strange
Reefs of silver into alabaster caves,
Golden buses, terracotta trains.

www.ingramcontent.com/pod-product-compliance
Lightning Source LLC
Chambersburg PA
CBHW062150100526
44589CB00014B/1762